ART LESSONS

ART LESSONS

POEMS BY ANN IVERSON

HOLY COW! PRESS :: DULUTH, MINNESOTA :: 2011

First printing: Fall, 2011.

Library of Congress Cataloging-in-Publication Data
Iverson, Ann.
Art lessons : poems / by Ann Iverson.
p. cm.
ISBN 978-0-9833254-2-0 (alk. paper)
1. Gogh, Vincent van, 1853-1890–Poetry. 2. Art–Poetry. I. Title.
PS3609.V47A89 2011
811'.6—dc22 2011011301

This project is supported in part by gifts from generous individual donors.

Holy Cow! Press books are distributed to the trade by:
Consortium Book Sales & Distribution, c/o Perseus Distribution, 1094 Flex Drive, Jackson, Tennessee 38301.

For personal inquiries, write to: Holy Cow! Press, Post Office Box 3170, Mount Royal Station, Duluth, Minnesota 55803.

Please visit our website: www.holycowpress.org

Printed in the United States of America.

ACKNOWLEDGEMENTS

THE AUTHOR WOULD LIKE TO THANK THE FOLLOWING PEOPLE
AND PUBLICATIONS:

A very special thanks to Kirsten Dierking in her visions for seeing the poems
within this book form a whole, also to Theresa Boyer, Carol Bjorlie,
Janet Jerve, Marie Rickmyer, Kathy Weihe, and Liz Weir, all who help keep
poetry in my life.

The painting in the author's photograph was recently installed at the
University of Minnesota Amplatz Children's Hospital.

"Into All Things We Enter" was inspired
by a photograph of Lake Superior by Dr. Ted Gundel

"Alms" and "Storm," *Talking Stick*, 2004

"Myopic Vision," *Dos Passos Review*, 2005

"Poppies," *Trillium Literary Journal*, 2007

"Wheat Field With Crows," *Asphalt Sky*, 2008

"Afraid to Sleep and Then Afraid to Wake," and "Today the World is Beautiful,"
The Taste of Permanence, 2008

"At the Foot of the Ozark Mountains," *Thanalonline Journal*, 2008
and *The Journal of World Culture and Literature*, 2011

"The Four O'clock Hour," *Pilgrimage* 2008

"Love," "Sunflowers," "After Painting," and "Solstice Nearing,"
Relief Magazine, 2008

"Art Lesson II," *Midway Journal*, 2008

"In Every Minute of Every Hour of Every Day,"
The Wind Blows, the Ice Breaks: Poems of Loss and Renewal by Minnesota Poets, 2010

"Landscapes," *The Saint Paul Almanac*, 2010

"All These Butterflies," "Reckless," "The Great Blue Heron," "To Know a Snow
Angel," *The Quiet Eye*, 2010

The poems listed below were written in response to large paintings of the same
title created by the author for her art exhibit Speaking Image at the Undercroft
Gallery, St. Mathew's Episcopal Church, April 2007. They also were published
along with the painting in *Trillium Literary Journal*, 2008:
"Reckless," "Together in the World," "Achilles Heal," "Moons of Jupiter,"
"Ladders to the Sun," and "Flowers for Daddy"

FOR MY SISTERS:

JEANNIE, CLAUDIA, MARGIE, MARY

Third Lesson

Final Lesson

First Lesson

There is nothing more artistic than to love others.
Vincent van Gogh

SUNFLOWERS

Oil on Canvas, 1888
VINCENT VAN GOGH

In 5th grade, the teacher handed out a brochure
from which to order prints of the classics for 99 cents.
My mother ordered several, among them your *Sunflowers*,
perhaps why we have these conversations.

Even in the print, the impasto was quite evident.
Though just 11 years old, I thought the vase
of the half way dying giants a bit peculiar, almost scary
like the tangling monsters in bad dreams.
But their floppy, golden heads made her happy,
and it made me happy to dutifully carry home
a new print every month in its tubular container
that we opened together on the kitchen table.

You painted them for Gauguin, who never made you happy,
but the *Sunflowers* must have spoken to you
of a life free of torment, one of complete elation,
a life where yellow holds the brush
and the eyes of life and death are equal in their beauty.

And Gauguin painted you painting them
as though the two of you followed in a circle
those nine autumn weeks in and out
of the yellow house in Arles
until the tragic took the canvas over.

I remember them in the living room
in their great oak frame she bought at the Salvation Army,
then again in the kitchen, and then again in the hall,
over her bed, and then back again to the living room.
Oh, she moved your flowers around so much,
and all I did was follow them around and her.

ACHILLES HEEL

Even if your mother,
sea nymph
with special powers,
lowers you slowly
hanging on
to your bitty heel
then dips you in
to a magical river,
you will never be
immortal.

Even when she finds
she forgot to soak
the heel she held you by,
your vulnerability
will follow,
your weaknesses inevitable.

Though for now, it's just
that one spot, tiny place
blazing out as a beam
to a world wild with torment,

even if she tries
to burn away the parts
that leave you open.

The Great Blue Heron

I love the great blue heron
who nests on my pond.

I love his stress
when red-winged black birds

peck at his head with retribution
for his thievery of eggs.

I love how he stands up and
takes it all,

the swirling wings
of tiny payback and I love, oh I love…

I love how the day exists beneath his wings
and even more

how they unfold: feather to muscle to bone
to flight and to somehow

I matter not in any of it.

Storm

The wolf howls a blue moon
and throws it to the sky
like the last of Van Gogh's
invading strokes of orange.

The final wails of the dying
can release the colors too.

Phone rings at 3:00 a.m.
What is real the receiver
does not know by heart.

This is for the mentally ill
the wild colors of their minds
the deep and lonesome country
friends and family wander.

To Know a Snow Angel

Is to love

what will wash away

with the wind

and drifted days.

Her wings will fade

so gently

into the blanched sky.

Deer might come to see

what has dissolved.

There are no lights

on a distant tree,

no sleigh bells,

no ringing of anything

anywhere.

Theory on Color

When we placed our mother
in the snow to rest
we dressed her in a purple sweater
for fear she would be chilled.
Our father stood behind
and gasped *my wife*.

That was 20 years ago.
Time has come and gone.
Some days have stayed too long
others gone too fast.

Her only sister still wears red,
though I never see her. News is
she takes classes at a local college,
but even that was years ago.

Two weeks before my mother died,
she lent me money for a coat.
She left with me in debt to her.
Of course that's how it went.

I tried to pay my father back
but he would not receive it.
Here, in fact, it's red, not green that lives.
And purple sings from silent snow.

Alms

Dawning on her
that it wasn't a public mass,
the homeless woman, sweet and slow of mind,
slipped out as unobtrusively
as she had slipped in
to sit at the front row of the Assumption Church,
closer to the altar than any of the family.

Between the homily and the eulogy,
she floated back in
and placed
a package of powdered donuts
on the pedestal
next to the urn
of my father's ashes.

Next to the man
who loved his pastries.
Beside the man
who always said *I'll make it up to you…*
Near the man
who never held his head too high.

Beside the man
whose mother
widowed, poor,
then finally drunk,
gave food to those with even less,
to me,
pennies off her dresser.

THE SCATTERING OF ASHES
For A

I am every cool breeze

and bite on the lake

when the fish follow

and the water reads your mind.

I am the tree of resolution

against a gray November sky.

I am the heart of the fleeting deer.

I follow the rolling hills at dusk

to the little fork in the road

where I'll find you in your dreams.

AFRAID TO SLEEP AND THEN AFRAID TO WAKE

Alone after the death of two fathers

That you might not open the morning first
or tighten the lid to the day.

Accustomed to you and feeling
in-comprehensible, though I know

if you were here, you would understand.
Innocent sounds enter the house and become

every fear I have. Our fathers walk together while I sleep.
One is pink and uncontrollable in Heaven.

The other is the last egg in a basket,
which God carries.

OLD LANGUAGE, NEW LIGHT

Nothing to say
the yellow finch
can't say better.

Nowhere to go
she hasn't gone

flitting

between cloud and sunlight
amid birch and oak

and alabaster light.
Follow me she says.

Stop and think for a moment,
then do.

Up here, you wouldn't
believe it:

a thesaurus of petals and color!

an unabridged sky
and reference to the world.

At this height I find the matching bracket
then sit down at a table of content.

Landmarks

for my parents

I The Cathedral

After Mass she made pot roast and potatoes
and we sat in silence at the harvest table.
What I didn't know is that all of her life
she tucked away pieces of palm
inside of drawers and books
pockets and glass knickknacks.
A certain kind of holiness
I keep finding years after her death
dusty, braided, frayed like the edges of a river.

II Sanitary Farm Dairies

The last of the real milkmen slowly go out.
When my father lost 35 years of pension from the
merger, he slowly raked the yard.
A two hour job took him all day;
he stopped often to take long drags
from generic cigarettes.
After she died, he stopped
tending the yard altogether;
the weeds grew up
as he sat in the corner of his kitchen
memorizing the small portrait
offered by the window.

III Downtown Saint Paul

Amazing then, at 48
I can wish myself
right back into her arms
as I did when she would leave
on Monday nights to shop
downtown Saint Paul.

From my bed, I would listen
for the click, click of her soft heels
on the sidewalk of an autumn night
the brush of packages against her coat.
In my life, have I ever felt more safe
than those evenings upon her return?

IV HARRIET ISLAND

Some people climbed the fence
and scaled the slanted rock
that keeps the mighty water contained.
I was afraid of the rushing darkness;
the under currents which would
take me in and swallow.
My mother in her navy blue turban
told me this was so.

V THE APPLE RIVER

One year I ate too many green grapes,
and got sick on the Apple River
which was close to the same year we found a bee
inside a can of shoe string potatoes.
We wrote a letter and sent it
with the evidence enclosed.
As compensation
we received a case of shoe string potatoes in the mail.
This was years before I would call my mother
from the phone at Woolworth's
saying that I would be late, a friend
had cut her hand on the glass of a display case
as my mother burst into a tearful mumble
that cousin David had frozen
found huddled in a wheat field.
His hands were in his pockets.

VI Harriet Island, Spring 1965

When the others had gone to Mass
at the Cathedral
shiny and domed up off the hill
we strolled the island
just the two of us
father and I
while the Mississippi
bent and lulled, groaned its size
a giant woken from a deep, deep sleep.

I was too small to notice the high water
in that year of great flooding
how the edge of the familiar
is swallowed by what is never known.
He reached into his pocket
for pennies and nickels
secretly dropped them on the grass
where, with my keen eyes, I would find them.
All of this before the pain of our lives
rose above sea level.

VII The Rock Garden

Father gathered rocks from
the shores of Lake Superior
back in the day when that wasn't illegal.
Mother planted snapdragons
under the complacent shade of birch.
I don't remember many words
exchanged between the two of them.

VIII First Ring Suburb

My parents bought their house for eight thousand dollars.
The old pond is no longer and it hasn't been for years.
We use to run through the field across the street and cry out
whiz whap; whiz whap.
The big city got bigger, and the mall goes under.
When my father had his stroke, we sold the house for sixty-seven.

When the mall was new, it had no roof.
We use to ride the carnival train, and I thought I'd never get home.
If it rained, we took a short cut through the alley.
At Pier One we bought oriental candies
with wrappers that melted on our tongues.
My sister worked at Heap Big Beef
which turned into an over-sized men's clothing store.
We wore our pajamas to the Coral Drive-in Theater while
Oscar's turned into J.T.'s and the malted milks perished.
Der Weiner-Schnitzel became a Taco Bell.
The nineteen cent coupons
that my mother clipped from *The Sun*
for a hot dog rolled in soft dough, expired.

IX Westchester Drive, 1968

No landscape which could
have shadowed your melancholy
no sea or mountain.
Nothing to come cascading in or down
to help you forget yourself completely.
Just the cat on your lap
and your polka dotted house dress
in bright green and hot pink
behind you a painting of a meadow.
If I may ask, who focused in on your sorrow?
Did you love his callused hands?
Did you love him then?

The Poppies

for C

My guess is, that I go unnoticed
in this world of opening and unfolding

still every morning
a few more disclose their dark prayer.

If I count the silent, there are exactly twelve.
I touch each one on the shoulder:

More gentle rain tonight.

I only did this worship the flower thing
because that winter brought so much death.

When he died in her bed
she moved weeping

from couch-to-bed-to-couch-to-floor
as though movement would suspend the pain

keep it floating above her
as a mare searching for shade

her skinny legs, collapsing and collapsing.
All I ever did was watch

wishing not for a prayer
but for something to say.

As if I could fold back
the frail petal of my tongue

and find *good news* just for her.

Drama

Here comes
the great blue heron

again

in the mystery ship
of his body

accurately
clattering

teasing
unleashing

the bone-wise hinge
of verticality

or trueness.

A curtain of reed opens
a horizontal

blue

finally alters the stage
as if you've landed

on your

life
but never knew it.

LOVE

Art is the only labour that succeeds by omission:
Between what we imagine and what's finally rendered
Is a world where only beautiful things that cannot exist are discovered.

—Jude Nutter

But love, too, is another labor
that propels itself in oversight.
How often we see our ways of loving wrong –
Have I, do I, will I

loved, love you well enough?
Once I thought love was a searching bird
flying in and out of my nest-like heart.
Or was it just a bird swooping to and from
my heart that had no likeness to its home?

In February the year after my father died
I painted twenty-three hearts
and sent them out like messenger pigeons.
Though I can rightly say I felt like I loved no one
which explains why none of them came back.

That was the year I thought of love
as a single tree without its leaves
in a blooming, ferocious jungle
that overlapped the boundaries
of what I've painted in my mind.
It stood there stark and useless
and I, a bird, looked on with shock and awe.

HORSES

for B and R

When she wheeled
her husband
to the pasture
where the sun shown
its best October face
when autumn air
breathed clear and bright
with understanding
her thoughts transformed to clouds
the shadowy and shifting light
of a new interpretation.

When the horses gathered
and put their noses to his bum arm
tongues to his soft head
to lick back what had been taken
a doorway opened and we entered.

We cross both thresholds with the horses.
Why would we not?

Their brazened glory
a cantor and a gallop
a swiftness in God's speed
a prideful gait towards horizons
whispering

We'll help you understand.

Second Lesson

Painting is a faith.
Vincent van Gogh

Myopic Vision

You went to church
three times a day
preached to potato farmers
clubbed and cut yourself
drank kerosene
saw color
and ate the blunted world.

Now we hang your pain
on freshly painted walls
or walls that have no hope
on walls that say
If you hang a painting
I will make you happy.

It works in our 24 x 36
poster-size world.
Vincent, I'm sorry
but it works.

WISH FOR CHILDHOOD

Who knew that wishing wasn't really a well
that swallowed the coins whole heartedly
doing the best it could in its deep amber dark
where we dropped our dreams with trust?

Who knew when we made a tent
of clothespins and blankets
slung over the line
that we would be forever
curators of our past?

I do not know now how much
my mother knew and did not know
though I continue out of her knowing
as though I am born again each day.

It's her calling out of words:
be home before dark
be careful with the boys
always believe in Jesus.

I wonder about this knowing:
That-knowing-the-knowing-in-between-
the-knowing-at-my-sides-the-knowing-in-and-out.

Is it the underrated tendencies of knowing
or the commitment to the other world
the summoned disposition
of all that becomes whole and pure?

Maybe it's just the words for the world that
seem wrong, a few notches off like

be careful what you wish for.

But never her favorite unabridged
calling out is wrong:

Always believe in Jesus
because he is your best friend.

Revision

No. Begin here.

That God is everywhere

you don't want him.

Nowhere when you do.

He is what falls of the shelf of your heart.
He is what puts the broken back together.

He is the vine you let grow in through the screen,
the thermometer of a tempered soul and wild.

Strike that out and try again.

Into All Things We Enter

Superior, ship-less
save one ghostly vessel

and one path of sun
towards a shore

beyond our knowing
a destination of light.

Seagulls not seen
or remembered

nor the passers-by
nor memory's intent.

Into all things we enter.
Into all things we become.

Into this calling
into this watery message.

This calm, this sane
on the verge of something

at the brink of brightness
of a land so emerald

you can hear it
gather at your feet.

Solstice Nearing

If you could see the sun as I do every morning,
stepping the horizon, not missing a rung,
its generous offering of saturated orange
beyond belonging or the obligatory.

If you could see the crescent moon as I do,
both of us quiet and dark in the undulating night
knowing it won't always be like this.
The moon will stay the same,
only turning its face from side to side,
but will never leave the orbit,
as you and I will, have to, and will.

Whichever way I'm going, I take the long way,
same road winding and curving through the trees
like the soul hovering over the place of death
then finally spinning off
into the contractual light that we call God.

People exist only in their minds and sense of duty
until the hint of the afterworld appears:
slight, unjust, promising and there.
When there are so many if's, too much can happen.

If the heart is strong enough.
If the moon is wise.
If heaven has a place.

At the Heart of the Garden

I want to say that I love God
though I no longer feel anything
but my fingers trembling
over the key board of a song.
To let it enter with admission
is an enigma of sorts.

What song does He sing without
the panel of notes that I have?
How do his fingers quake
over the light of our joint failures?

What is it that He does
at the heart of the garden of light?
From which energy expands its course
from which love relinquishes the day
as the minutes quaver beyond.

The Resurrection

Good Friday

Tonight the world is as quiet as cotton,
the air as still as a womb.
And I am here trying to amend my past with God.
My back is sore and feet asleep.
My soul is pacing the hall.
There is nothing I can do to change this hour.

There is no lark to sing the heavens better
than this desire to be holy.

Holy Saturday

Once I felt I knew God so well that he was able to break open my heart.
Tap, tap, tap and then His fist through my door
only to find me needing Him.
There are arms in this life that will never hold me.
There are times in this life when I know that they are His.

Easter Morning

I wake to a dream of doing impossible tasks of love.
The silence again and then I rise.
There are heights I know nothing of.
There are stars that shine in the day.
Once I held a list of things in my heart for many years.

THE ILLUMINATED BIBLE

The St John's Bible
Minneapolis Institute of Arts

The bird carries the mistakenly omitted
on a silken thread
tucks it into place, so the Lord's word
provides promise: what has gone wrong
can be retrieved with beak and wing.

When I loved God, I loved Him
there was no omission,
no misunderstanding.

Now if I love God or not, I can't tell.
Is this wrong? Will you send
a little bird to mend my faith in you?

WHILE PAINTING, ARS POETICA IN WINTER

So bitterness is not olive
but scarlet and with wings.
I watch it dart away
through birch and bleeding sky.

Anger is impossible to mix.
The sleeping dogs agree.
They run through yellow, orange
prairie – dreamy dreams.

The sky becomes a blend of shadow
never made from dark
while set free ghosts
run rampant through the snow.

Mistakes evolve to splendor.
All winter
only beauty answers my call.

I Have Known for Years

Though never understood the trickle of your smile
in weary times, your cascading dimples against all odds
assuredness in simplicity and the dome of angels
that circle round your head.

I have known for years your distant glance
but not the misconceptions of your beauty now
that fall to me for memory's sake,
a waterfall of neither water nor air.

I comprehend your gravity
and how you let it go.
I demonstrate its purpose
by waking every day
walking on this earth.

In the levels of heaven,
you are the moon right now
but someday I will be the ribbon
that floats you from above.

LADDERS TO THE SUN

We all need one or two
or three or four
okay, several ladders to the sun
so all our friends can come along
as we raise our legs and brace our arms
for this magnificent climb to light.

Nothing can hinder us
as we leave behind our cloudy lives
depart our hazy ways
as glory proves
the closer we get
to be in every corner
shining through every rung
every step
everywhere and anywhere.

I'm not really talking about Heaven.
No, today it's just the sun.

Searching

I did not feel
the hand of God on my life

so I went down to the swamp and reeds,
down to a promise of the wild.

Only found that no one had been there,
witnessed that nothing had changed.

The snow still cliché.
The pheasant still anxious in its dart.

The trees a metaphor for anything
moot and mixed

an avalanche of birds flocking in
to their weighted branches.

So I pulled aside
and started to pluck

my eyebrows
in the rearview mirror

anything to take control
anything to make a difference.

Clean arches over
the waters to my soul.

And it was in the
right river there

and only there
I saw Him rowing.

in Medias Res

Lord, how did you bring me
to this hour of in-between?

Not near the beginning,
not near the end

the blessed ways of *in the midst*
as a doe at the flank

of the wild
and bordered gardens

her trembling stalls to pull up
the lupine, leave a print

of the insatiable to satisfy
as she walks calmly to the place

she knows is best for her
while the woman in the window

calls to her
once more.

Third Lesson

I am still far from being what I want to be.
Vincent van Gogh

THE FIRST VINCENT VAN GOGH

So Mrs. Van Gogh
delivered him dead.

Few know this story.

Few words for this.
It must be a quiet mum

for carrying
life and death

simultaneously.

Out of all of what
can happen

this is truly
the one thing I can't bear.

ART

Cannot replace a baby
nor rip a heart in shreds.

Cannot bring back the dead
nor make a person wholly happy.

Ah, yes, the temporary glint
of the stallion chased.

But in what circumstance
do we ever catch up?

Cannot replace a god.
There must be a higher power

than this emptiness
in my hands.

GOD TO ADAM

You won't notice my taking
or that a part of you is gone.

At dawn, you will recognize
yourself in her.

But this part of you
will no longer be accessible.

After centuries of being with her
you will, for one moment,

realize why I did it this way.
But then suddenly insight will fly out

as a sparrow
darting through bright air.

ALL THESE BUTTERFLIES

after Auden's "Musee des Beaux Arts"

About happiness,
they are never wrong

as one seemed
to love me all day long

as I worked the lonesome
acres of this land.

Perhaps my sweat
was the attraction

as it kept landing
on my shoulder

darting towards
my heart

twinkling
with desire.

The plunge and readiness
for nectar, the succulent

bead on the
heat of my skin

mistaken for
hibiscus.

Of evasion, they are genius.
Congregation too, a multiplicity

of worlds, the introvert
the extrovert,

explaining why all of them
didn't flutter up and follow.

And in some world,
I thought I deserved that.

Spare

after Akmahtova

The memory of sun
weakens in my heart.

The moon regards
her collateral light.

When you said
say something honest

I searched my weary bag
found nothing but stars

with dole beyond expression.

How half shed
we have become

you maybe to light
me at half to darkness.

~

The wind warm, then torrid.
No bodies of light
volunteer a cure.

Even snowdrifts
in their wished–washed ways
remain undecided.

The suitor comes to me
in dreams.
The easy touching of these hands

singing what was said
against the red – the pink
remains unchallenged.

One luminary shines
in a garden of snow

The cat prowls
on the ledge of light.
Shadows prophesy.

We listen.

The great river does not flow ahead.
The prediction of ours

– is silence –

greater than the country fields
wider than the ocean
deeper than the mighty sea.

~

We weary so,
pull out the place
of sleep too soon.
Your sleepy confidence
captivates
even minor shadows.

Language exists
to fill the hollow night.

I want nothing from you
Because there is nothing
of yours
that is not mine.

Not even your glances,
not even
The Ghost of the first days
which came to us…

~

What is in your broad shoulders
and shadows that they cast
but do not see?

And even now I find
that in those arms,

I have relented.

What is it then
that I have to offer from
the spare? Yet –

He whose look will be directed
Into my eyes, at once will see it whole.

~

If I dwindle along the lane
of what was us,
may the power enter
as it might not enter you.

It's only my way
of remembering:
footsteps
we made on the sidewalks
of the city, to and fro.

Now
down country roads
both walking
in a silence half-lost.

~

Each time we do not speak
I cloak silence as lichen on stone.

Heavier though
As the path I push
Through woods,
Scrapple with the then.

How I finally settle
On the unsettled
Rain of that which
I have sung more than once.

Voiceless we are and were.
If we wanted something more
Then we should have been.

WALTER REED ARMY MEDICAL FACILITY

December, 2009 for RJ

Early morning, I gather soft murmurs on the hotel shuttle:

The first surgery nicked his colon, ten more after that
His dad left on Saturday
Mom leaves on Sunday
A sister leaves Wednesday
An aunt arrives on Thursday

—

Inside every heart, there's a painting, one of oil never drying.
Inside these walls are portraits of life impossible to render.

—

One canvas offers:
an Army Champlain around a make-shift altar in the jungle;
one chopper hovers overhead.
The soldiers' hands are folded, heads bowed.
If there is a silence beyond silence, here it is.

—

As though on skateboards,
legless boys cruise the grounds on electronic devices.
Sisters and mothers chase them.
Someone tries to tell me the left leg is target,
key seat in the hummer, but I see the right gone too.
I see the middle of nowhere.
I see the nothingness.
I digest the cost for freedom.

—

These days the wound is left open until signs of infection are gone.
I wish you could cut the heart open, mend it
then let it drain and dry for days in the sun.

—

Second canvas provides: a priest washing a soldier's feet.
Some days, I think there is nothing holy left.
But if there is a holy beyond holy, I'll take it in.

—

We lie on soft mats with soldiers in meditation.
She tells us to forget about ourselves,
introduces us to each part of our being.
I whispered to myself no more war poems. I told myself that.

WAR POEM

Since we came to this field with pain
is this the path where love should end?

As wild lupine diminish
and secrets of the garden unfold.

What is told is mostly sorrow.
We filled this prairie with so much sorrow.

We took our hands
and threw grief to the wild.

It took it for a while, but then the deer
who once came, left for good.

Their sudden darting disappeared.
Even the bunnies are now just clay

a statuary of their lives
before we entered.

At the Foot of the Ozark Mountains

Two monarchs catch themselves
merge involuntarily into motion and the swirl.

Curved and synergistic the road asks
only that we don't forget.

The mountains gone now
on the page before
plead too
with the cattle peaceful
in their paragraphs.

How could I?
With the wild yellow flowers
impossibly at ease
like sentinels at the base
of a huge idea
to save the world?

Learning How to Paint the Clouds

Every day the same constant longing,

yet an unfamiliar, unnoticed shifting

as the trees remind of every journey.

And even though they have never traveled very far,

the trees, and I know that this untrue,

for their branches reach beyond

and they know their swelling roots so well,

and the last of their tiniest branches stretch for the sky.

They live in both worlds and understand

their hair turning in all the hues.

Yet they are never shocked when so much changes,

will never find themselves frantic

even when the winds shake and storm,

they never lose themselves.

But the clouds just keep shifting, shaking, moving.

SOMETIMES

Sometimes love
makes me sad,

sad as a luminary out
beside the other lit.

Sad as water is in dark,
offering no reflection anywhere.

I search for other things,
I do.

Varying forms and content
take me elsewhere.

Sometimes when I am opened
I am a stem of milkweed

without the pure flowing
goodness of white.

When love, loves itself

and not me,
it's always then

I feel a blanket of air
tossed over by a stranger.

Garden Reverie W/Miss Bishop

With melody, deep, clear, and liquid slow
and, the brazen path of history
enter this gateway
of bentwood
of alabaster prayer.
What gift do you have for your hands?
Like the promise of air to lung
or the trill of birds to morning?
Find your way among
the over grown past.
Give your soul to passing clouds.
Engage in the industry of sky.
Forget your
heart that sinks through fading colors deep.

(first and last lines from Elizabeth Bishop)

After Painting

Red is making love
and yellow stands for birth.
Plum is the color of a baby.

Turquoise is that old idea,
the lip of the can on a shelf
just waiting to say it all over again.

Green is an argument and consequently blue
after it's been washed over
in my mind for all these years.

Moons of Jupiter

Metis is the closest moon to Jupiter.
Leda is the smallest.

Europa is large and dense and icy
so I won't be going there.

Thebe offers dust to the Gossamer ring
how kind of her and beautiful.

Adrastea orbits faster than her father
leaves the big one spinning.

Imagine that. Amalthea gives off more
heat than she receives. Who could be

so sacrificial? Himalia is quiet.
No one knows too much, except she's

number 10, not here, but in the sky.
Callisto's face is scarred with craters

and ejecta. Okay whatever.
Galileo found IO spewing molten color,

just like me with paints, out of control
and in another orbit.

Ganymede is magnetic and thus
attracts me so, while Carme orbits

opposite like a retrograde
in action. Lysithea is eleven.

Elara number twelve. Maybe you
could name your children after them.

They just keep spilling out, and poor
Jupiter can't keep control. He can't consider

all the rest. I suppose their names too hard
to pronounce, their lives too difficult to manage.

Step Mother

With the window half open
she hears part of the view.

And interestingly enough

when all is said and done
she is still herself.

Everything else is what it is.
She only sees a few sounds.

~

With the window wide open
she sings in a voice not hers

yet captivatingly sound.

She wears another's clothes.
Looks goods. Looks good.

They fit her well. In the mirror
she is pleased and shimmers.

TOGETHER IN THE WORLD

Whatever shape we take
we are together in the world.

And through uncharted waters
energies arise, give power.

We learn to swirl and dip and dance,
survive the oceans of our lives

as bodies of blue floating and bobbing
in love and all its channels.

Under currents threaten,
but see the light behind?

No need to feel the tow.
See us touching? Letting go?

See the colors swirling round us?
You and I, together in the world.

LAST LESSON

The best way to know God is to love many things.
VINCENT VAN GOGH

WHEATFIELD WITH CROWS

Vincent van Gogh, oil on canvas, 1890

Some say it was your note to us:
the crows and crooked roads
a rotating light of spirit
tunneling down the path
of which there are three choices:

It bears study
the uncontrolled violence
of both color and paint.

~

Speculations hinge on whether the crows
are flying towards the painter
or away from him.

~

His perceptions towards nature
may have darkened.

It's all been said one way or another
under a turbulent sky
where they argue back and forth
about what you may or may not have meant.

Yet you walked yourself back to the
Ravoux Inn where you finally collapsed,
your final gesture.
Nothing more.
Nothing less.

But for now let's just agree
it was only the sun breaking through
or a cloud wafting by
and an eagle covered in glory
flying off the canvas.

THE FOUR O'CLOCK HOUR

for T

My bi-polar friend lives on Sunny View Lane.
Most days, he finds his way home
to the place where he shines with such brilliance.

It's the Four O'clock hour in winter
the hour, not hollow, not full

the hour when questions are asked
and answers *consider* the question.

The hour that moon dips
from the-very-best-bucket-of-white

and all the shades of
and all the shades after
and before
of light and bright follow.

He says *the scientists say*
there is more dark in the world
than light.

Scientists speak of matter-energy-orbits.

I speak of energy-orbits-matter.
Consider all the good hearts of the world

and multiply that by light. Let that
be your equation.

May that be the moment
we must look away

or be blinded by the sun.

In Every Minute of Every Hour of Every Day

All winter long and then some into early spring
either the moon or the sun followed or led the way.

And in every minute when they divulge
their round and serious request

between collected branch and cloud
I understand that I am needed

to sweep their petals of light which fall around my steps
to provide focus for them so far away

to find words for a friend's life broken,
to clean time's closet where so much is stored of every hour.

And I try to consider how life works.
And I try to consider how I fit in to this extraordinary plan.

And sometimes with a troubled mind
(but not always) I find no resolution.

So in the mirror I apply bright red lips
to this portrait of a woman, considering and considering.

And sometimes I look over to the other side
and see myself and know that in the

sweet-sad-coming-and-going
of-every-minute-of-every-hour-I-have-changed.

Reckless

In every heart there is
a reckless summon
calling us
from ordinary
delivering us
from order
saving us
from certainty.

Is there a problem
with chaos?

Look at the daisies
along the bay
scattered haphazardly
for a good stretch of mile
like hippies at a sit down.

One week they are there,
the next gone.

Who would mow down
this mob?

Who would
thrash the principle?

All of us need more often
to turn up wild in a field.

Season

I've been making the sign of the cross
at least three times a day.

In the car, at the store, near my desk:
forehead, heart, left shoulder, right.

I took the black lab's paws
and helped her form her own

cross to bare:

forehead, heart, left shoulder, right.

We Buried Her in the Field

We buried her in the field at dusk, two days before Thanksgiving.
The field where wild lupine grows in spring, where oaks extend their hands.

Every gesture from the nearing forest came to enter with us.
Her body sleek and withered, eyes glossed with death's perfection.

And she had no apologies to make.
She had burned no bridges.

~

So you ask of the sky *Is there a right thing to do*?
It doesn't answer. We put her down by needle.

~

Is there anything natural or unnatural about the dark?
When it's time, we bound towards it.
After we patted the dirt and repositioned the earth,
I thought about lying down in the weeds beside her grave.

~

We buried her in the field where she danced and leapt the briar
came tumbling back a mess of gratitude.

Is there relief when you say goodbye, one last time, to the face of happiness?

Never.

November in the Country

after they put the second dog to rest, the men sped off to go further into the woods

after she scurried to purge the house of grief

after she found that when she looked in the closet for something to wear

after she found that when she looked in the closet for something to take with her

after she looked in the closet to find something worth putting on

after she fumbled with her hair and a necklace and a blouse

after she saw her face in the mirror

before-and-ever-after-&-during-enduring-&-enduring.

THE DEPOSITION OF DREAMS

Missing sleep is not advisable;
There is too much drama in the dream
World that requires your attention.

Horoscope

You didn't sleep through the interrogation. You were wide awake for it
sitting on the edge of your bed when you saw yourself dreaming

of your father's ghost standing silently in the closet
between your winter coats and his regret for never being enough.

Frightened, you tried to push his foaming light down the stairs.
Though he never lunged or raised a hand. Never.

What circumstance in your life might shepherd him through the veil?
This helpful, misinterpreted ghost, shy and waiting in the shadows
of wool and buttons.
The night before, when life was hard, you tucked his photo
into the pocket of your long grey coat.

You didn't plan for his appearance; you didn't foresee the questions.
You didn't expect this small secret ceremony

of a wakeful grace
from the living dead.

AUTUMNAL

Tell the trees to wait for us
before they set themselves on fire.

Tell the wind to settle down;
the leaves are happy where they are.

Invite the moon to visit
with all the gossip of the sky.

Tell the night to leave the room.
Put darkness in its place.

Tell the woman who wants to leave
tell her something, make her stay.

BRIDGES

for S

I'm watching a woman wearing a hat
walking slowly, but determinedly

up over the arc of an old stone bridge.
At either end are Monet's gardens.

Though she doesn't know this
cannot see what I see

in this imaginary place of in-between
where I've watched

other women walk bridges, build bridges,
burn bridges,
away from me, towards me,

with love or despair
swinging in a basket at their sides.

As she walks, something flows
from her scarf, now just dots of paint.

Lilies or pansies?
Daffodils or clover?

It's hard to tell
from where I am

at one end, staying
until I see the last turn of her head

the last wave of her hand
the last promenade

until I know she's happy
until I see she's made it safe.

FLOWERS FOR DADDY

Because I forgot how long it's been,
something said to paint you flowers.

So I did, but even the act of art
even the gesture of clumsy daisies

in a nicked up, gaudy frame won't bring us
any closer. When you lived, you were distant

though it didn't make me love you less.
When she passed, you were far flung

far off, though only minutes away.
Still it didn't lessen love.

Nor do always love's lessons enlighten
except for when memories collide.

You up there, me here. It was five years after
wasn't it? When you finally

let me in to take down and wash her flow blue
china. An afternoon together, a stepping stool

and coffee, me at the sink, sleeves rolled up, you
at the kitchen table. This room I keep inside

of me for you, is hazy, not awkward like
these flowers, six, of course, there are exactly six.

TONIGHT I WISH FOR DEER

for my parents

and a feast with phantoms
on a downy cove, amidst

the naked birch, among the
darkest leaves of oak.

Yes, I'd like to dine
with the dead tonight

but not have them be alive
again. For how could they

ever forgive me
for this wish so strong

it pulls them
from their rest.

ART LESSON

stay away from black
use only white
mix it with everything you have.

I did that
but the paint dried
into words.

Blue became even *bluer than*

red setting its sight on being
broken hearted that

I kept mixing to find more words.
Green *chose to be the field.*

More pastures; a better way to graze.

Yellow designated *sun will inspire*

red and hues unimaginable
to the secret, sacred eye.

One Life

And in it I have made small beauties here and there.
And in it I have held in my mouth unnecessary words.
I then have opened it again: wrongfully, regretfully.

I have made out of words an empty bowl and then again
have built a prosperous city.

I have stumbled through small wreckage, have watched the heart
descend into dark doors, then ascend through open windows.
I have calculated life as a falling and rising bank account
for which I do not have the code.

But have I not risked for the sake of love?

Did I not hold in my palm my father's dehydrated fingers
as he bore the long length of nursing home death?

Five years in a wheel chair: mute, immobile, sores to the bone.
And did he not, with his one good hand, brush my hair aside
as I bent to wash his privacies?

Did he not, in his last days, bend towards me in a slobbery kiss?

All I can come up with are words.

In them I bless the syllables.
In them I form the shape of a heart
from paint and vowels and consonants.

TODAY THE WORLD IS BEAUTIFUL

Today the world is beautiful
even amidst the dark

even amongst the broken-down
and washed-up dreams.

Today the world is clear as a bell
regardless of confusion

not considering
the undefined.

Today the world is what it is
or how we see it

despite the harshness and the squalor
in the face of numbness and debasement.

Today the world is extraordinary
as the birdless sky shifts

and glimpses of goodness
pass over and fears subside.

Today the world provides days
to spring ahead.

We store daylight
like books on a shelf

all the openings and the closings
all the lovely pages turning back and forth.

And the sun, plentiful
and dignified, washes over.

Art Lesson II

You saturate the canvas, turn it upside down,
scrape the color off, turn it again
as if changing the view might change the circumstance.

You fight a small illness and dream of painting
a fish in a true-blue-ocean
where you find an animal with eyes so olive and loving
every discrepancy becomes congruent.

The truth is that everything is abstract space making one thing whole.
The human eye, for instance, when magnified

is merely a collection of space and shape
while some call it the portal to the soul.

I painted eggs floating in a dark space but really moons
in a beckoning orbit.
I painted them moons, not embryos.

Under these stars and layers of light
the sky must grant permission to the heart's deepest letter.

What you haven't given away
but want to.

What you can no longer keep
but must.

About the Author

Ann Iverson is the author of *Come Now to the Window* (Laurel Poetry Collective, 2003) and *Definite Space* (Holy Cow! Press, 2007). She is a graduate of both the MALS and the MFA programs at Hamline University. Her poems have appeared in a variety of journals and venues including Writer's Almanac with Garrison Keillor. As a visual artist, she enjoys the integrated relationship between the visual image and the written image. Her art work has been featured in two art exhibits as well as at the University of Minnesota Amplatz Children's Hospital.